Can You Tell an Ostrich from an Emu?

Buffy Silverman

Lerner Publications Company

Minneapolis

Lerner Publications Company
A division of Lerner Publishing Group, Inc.
241 First Avenue North
Minneapolis, MN 55401 U.S.A.

Website address: www.lernerbooks.com

Library of Congress Cataloging-in-Publication Data

Silverman, Buffy.
    Can you tell an ostrich from an emu? / by Buffy Silverman.
       p. cm. — (Lightning bolt books™—animal look-alikes)
    Includes index.
    ISBN 978-0-7613-6741-3 (lib. bdg. : alk. paper)
    1. Ostriches—Juvenile literature. 2. Emus—Juvenile literature. I. Title.
 QL696.S9S55 2012
 598.5'24—dc23   2011025545

Manufactured in the United States of America

1 — PP — 12/31/11

Table of Contents

From Head to Toe

Ostriches and emus look a lot alike. They are both very large birds. Like all birds, they have feathers. But ostriches and emus cannot fly. Instead, they run on long, strong legs.

Can you guess which animal is an ostrich and which is an emu?

The feathers on ostriches and emus are soft and loose. The birds look shaggy.

This photo shows what an emu's feathers look like close-up.

Both ostriches and emus have long necks. Their necks tower above tall grass. And the birds' huge eyes watch for enemies.

This emu has a long neck and large eyes.

But you can tell these big birds apart. Look at this ostrich's head. Only a few fuzzy feathers grow on its head. You can see its pink skin.

Dark feathers cover an emu's head. Its feathers blend in with grass and bushes.

Count the toes on this ostrich's feet.

Each foot has two toes.

The ostrich's big toe has a long, sharp nail. No nail grows on its little toe. Ostriches run and kick with their big, strong feet.

This small toe has no nail.

An emu has three toes on
each foot. Long nails grow
on all three toes.

Emus use their sharp
toenails to fight enemies.

Feathers and Wings

Black and white feathers on male ostriches make the males easy to spot. Female and young ostriches are harder to see. Their gray or brown feathers blend in with tall grass.

This is a male ostrich.

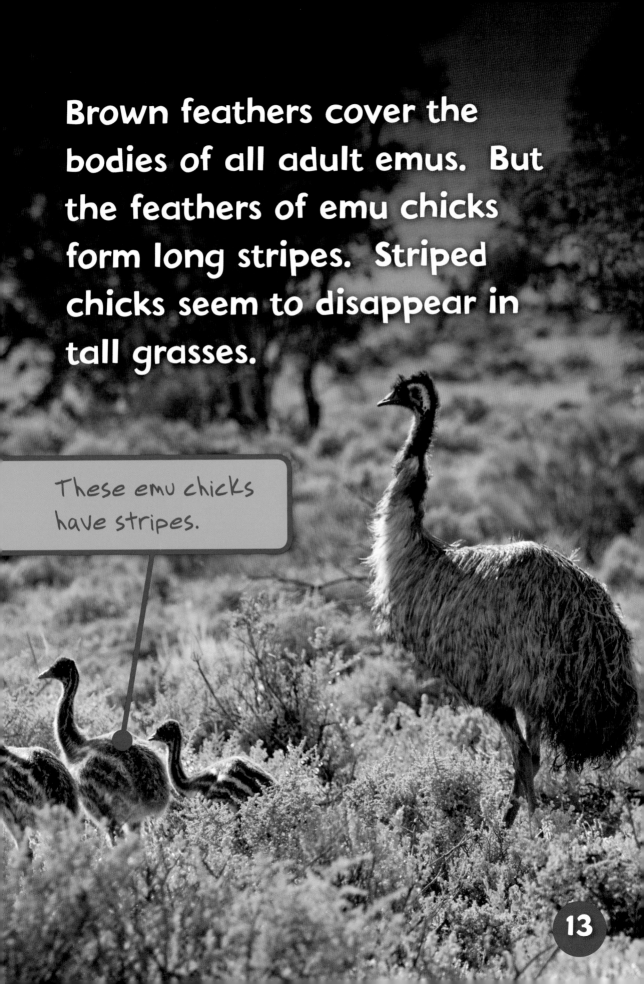

Brown feathers cover the bodies of all adult emus. But the feathers of emu chicks form long stripes. Striped chicks seem to disappear in tall grasses.

These emu chicks have stripes.

These chicks keep cool under a huge ostrich wing.

Ostriches spread their huge wings to balance themselves when they run. Their wings can also keep sun and rain off their chicks. Male ostriches lift their big wings to show off for females.

Emu wings are tiny. Thick feathers cover them. An emu spreads its wings when it is hot. That helps it cool off.

This emu's wing is much smaller than an ostrich's wing.

Egg Time

A male ostrich hisses at another male. He tells him to stay away. Then the male ostrich scrapes a hole in the ground with his feet. Three to five females will lay their eggs there.

A female emu calls to a male. Her call sounds like a beating drum. The call tells a male emu to build a nest. He builds the nest with bark, sticks, leaves, and grass.

Male emus build a nest on the ground using items such as twigs and grass.

An ostrich nest holds fifteen to sixty huge eggs. The female sits on the eggs during the day. She keeps them warm. At night, the male sits on them.

A female emu lays five to fifteen eggs. She leaves the nest after she lays her eggs. Other females will lay more eggs there. The male stays and cares for the eggs. He doesn't even leave to get food for eight weeks. Finally, the chicks hatch.

A male emu turns the eggs in a nest.

Ostrich chicks hatch in about six weeks. They leave the nest a few days later. The chicks travel with both parents. Their parents keep them safe.

This ostrich chick hatches from an egg.

Three-day-old emu chicks also leave their nest. Their dad follows them. He shows the chicks where to find food. He kicks away enemies with his strong legs.

Where In the World?

Ostriches live in Africa. They live in dry, sandy places.

This ostrich runs in Africa. Ostriches once lived in Asia and the Middle East too, but people hunted them and they died off.

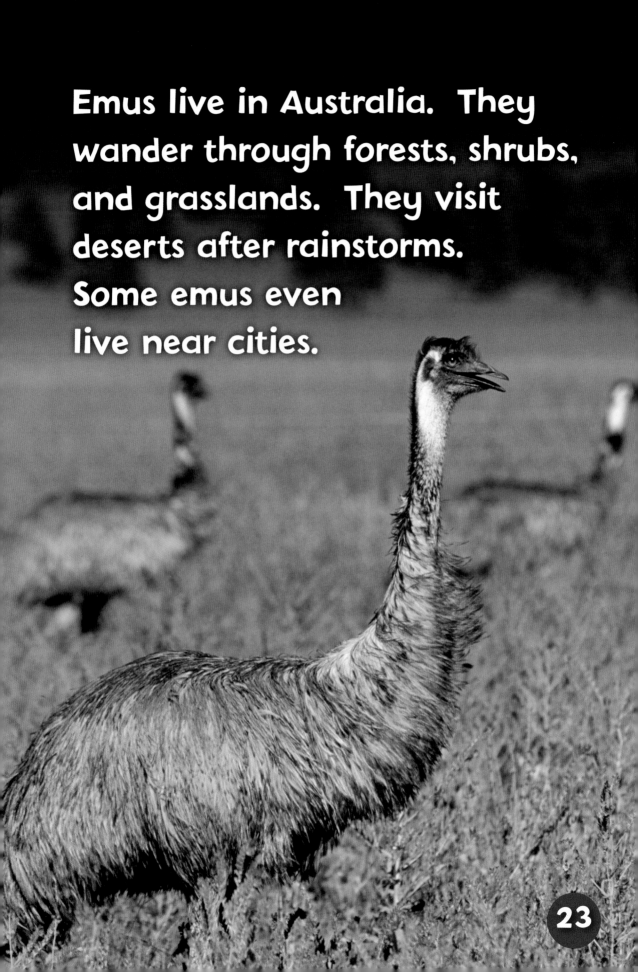

Emus live in Australia. They wander through forests, shrubs, and grasslands. They visit deserts after rainstorms. Some emus even live near cities.

Ostriches live in groups. About ten ostriches usually stay together. Sometimes flocks of one hundred or more gather.

A flock of ostriches gathers at a waterhole near giraffes, zebras, and antelope.

Emus usually live alone. But flocks form where emus find food. They feast on seeds, fruits, and insects. Flocks can travel far, following the rain. Emus need to drink water every day.

Ostriches graze on seeds and roots. They also catch insects and lizards. Ostriches often feed with zebras and antelopes. Ostriches can go for days without water.

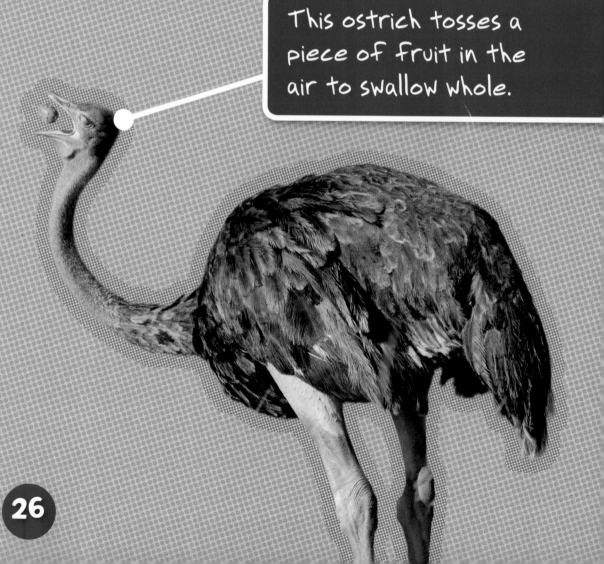

This ostrich tosses a piece of fruit in the air to swallow whole.

Ostriches race across sand
and grass. Emus run past
shrubs and trees.

Can you tell these
look-alikes apart?

Who Am I?

Look at the pictures below. Which ones are ostriches? Which ones are emus?

 Dark feathers cover my head.

My head has few feathers.

 Large wings help me keep my balance.

I spread my tiny wings to cool off.

 I live in Australia.

I live in Africa.

Fun Facts

- Ostriches are the largest birds in the world. Male ostriches reach 9 feet (2.7 meters) tall. That's taller than the world's tallest man. Female ostriches grow more than 6 feet tall (1.9 m).

- Emus are the world's second-largest birds. An adult emu grows up to 6 feet (1.8 m). Female emus are bigger than males. Some are as tall as basketball players.

- Ostriches flop down when there is danger. They stretch their heads and necks flat on the sandy ground. Only their dark bodies can be seen. From far away, it looks as if their heads have disappeared!

- Emus shake their tail feathers when enemies are near. The feathers make a rattling sound. Emus race away from danger. They also jump high. An emu can jump 7 feet (2.1 m).

Glossary

bird: an egg-laying animal with feathers and wings

chick: a baby bird

desert: a dry, sandy place with little rainfall. Plants and animals that live in a desert survive with little water.

flock: a group of birds that lives, travels, and feeds together

grassland: land where mostly grass grows

graze: to eat plants, or to eat small amounts of food throughout the day

hatch: to break out of an egg

Further Reading

Berkes, Marianne. *Over in Australia: Amazing Animals Down Under.* Nevada City, CA: Dawn Publications, 2011.

Creature Features: Ostriches
http://kids.nationalgeographic.com/kids/animals/creaturefeature/ostrich

Flightless Bird Pictures
http://animals.nationalgeographic.com/animals/photos/flightless-bird-photos

San Diego Zoo's Animal Bytes: Emu
http://www.sandiegozoo.org/animalbytes/t-emu.html

Silverman, Buffy. *Do You Know about Birds?* Minneapolis: Lerner Publications Company, 2010.

Stout, Frankie. *Ostriches: Nature's Biggest Birds.* New York: PowerKids Press, 2009.

Index

Photo Acknowledgments

The images in this book are used with the permission of: © Eric Isselé/Shutterstock.com, p. 1 (top); © Tier und Naturfotografie/SuperStock, pp. 1 (bottom), 13; © NaturePL/SuperStock, p. 2; © Minden Pictures/SuperStock, pp. 4 (left), 15, 19, 28 (middle right); © Isselee/Dreamstime.com, p. 4 (right); © David Lee/Shutterstock.com, p. 5; © Larry Williams/CORBIS, p. 6; © Anup Shah/Photolibrary, pp. 7, 28 (top right); © Christopher Meder Photography/Shutterstock.com, pp. 8, 28 (top left); © Arco Images GmbH/Alamy, p. 9; © Til Vogt/Shutterstock.com, p. 10; © Alain Mafart-Renodier/Photolibrary, p. 11; © NHPA/SuperStock, p. 12; © Jorens-Belde/Photolibrary, pp. 14, 28 (middle left); © Anup Shah/naturepl.com, p. 16; © Cyril Ruoso/Photolibrary, p. 17; © Joe McDonald/CORBIS, p. 18; © Karin Duthie/Alamy, p. 20; © Jeffery Drewitz/Cephas Picture Library/Alamy, p. 21; © Armands Pharyos/Alamy, pp. 22, 28 (bottom right); © Boris Karpinski/Alamy, pp. 23, 28 (bottom left); © Clem Haagner/Photo Researchers, Inc., p. 24; © Earl & Nazima Kowall/CORBIS, p. 25; © Philip J. Briggs/Alamy, p. 26; © Animals Animals/SuperStock, p. 27 (top); © John Carnemolla/CORBIS, p. 27 (bottom); © pandapaw/Shutterstock.com, p. 30; © nadi555/Shutterstock.com, p. 31.

Front cover: © Peter Betts/Shutterstock.com (top); © Sgoodwin4813/Dreamstime.com (bottom).

Main body text set in Johann Light 30/36.